Accelerated Christian Training Series

Laying the FOUNDATION

BOOK 5

THE NEW COVENANT

978 0768421460

D1652129

Dr. Mark Hanby

Destiny Image® Publishers, Inc.
P.O. Box 310
Shippensburg, PA 17257-0310

"Speaking to the Purposes of God for This
Generation and for the Generations to Come"

ISBN 0-7684-2146-2

For Worldwide Distribution
Printed in the U.S.A.

This book and all other Destiny Image, Revival Press,
MercyPlace, Fresh Bread, Destiny Image Fiction,
and Treasure House books are available
at Christian bookstores and distributors worldwide.

For a U.S. bookstore nearest you, call **1-800-722-6774**.
For more information on foreign distributors,
call **717-532-3040**.
Or reach us on the Internet: **www.destinyimage.com**

Contents

Introduction

And you shall know the truth, and the truth shall make you free (John 8:32).

What Is Truth?

Truth Is a Person

"What is truth?" Pilate asked Jesus (Jn. 18:38). The answer to Pilate's timeless question was standing before him. Truth is not a series of facts or the sum of information. Truth is a Person: Jesus Christ. Jesus said of Himself, "I am the way, the truth, and the life" (Jn. 14:6). Truth is not only rational, it is relational. Religious theory that only teaches about God can never liberate the soul. True freedom is found in knowing Him. "And ye shall know the truth, and the truth shall make you free" (Jn. 8:32).

God has chosen to unfold His relational truth in various ways throughout the Bible and always in the form of personal relationship between Himself and men such as Adam, Noah, and Abraham. The unfolding revelation of God's relationship with man was spelled out in agreements between God and man called covenants. What better way to unfold a relational truth than in the context of relationship?

Truth Is the Result of Seeking Jesus

This relational truth is more than experience. Despite his great experience on the road to Damascus, the apostle Paul did not end his search for truth but wrote, "...that I may know *Him* and the power of His resurrection, and the fellowship of His sufferings..." (Phil. 3:10, emphasis mine). Job, wounded and in distress, cried out, "Oh that I knew where I might find *Him*..."

(Job 23:3). Jesus said, "Blessed are those who hunger and thirst for righteousness, for they shall be filled" (Mt. 5:6). Our finding the truth is the result of a hunger to know the Person of Jesus Christ. We do not seek truth and find Jesus; we seek Jesus and find the truth.

Truth Is a Highway

We may think of truth as a highway—an endless journey into the Person of God. All of us walking in the light of relationship with God are at some point in that journey. As we "seek the Lord" and "search the Scriptures," we advance. The **A**ccelerated **C**hristian **T**raining **S**eries has been created to help us move on in that journey into the Lord regardless of whether we are new believers or seasoned saints of God. There is always more truth for us regardless of our place along the road. "His ways [are] past finding out" (Rom. 11:33b).

It is important that every believer follow a course such as this. Although the believer may be exposed to a variety of good biblical preaching, there must be a systematic seeking after truth to provide a foundation upon which to grow in relationship with the Person of Jesus. Imagine agreeing to marry someone of whom you had only seen a pencil sketching. It is our intention in this course of seeking to paint a full and vital portrait of the Christ who is alive in you.

If you are a new traveler on the highway of truth, you have begun the most exciting journey of your life. Many parallels can be drawn between the new believer and a newborn child. It would be a criminal act to leave an infant out in the cold or in a house without someone to give him attention and care. It is likewise a tragedy when the Church does not nurture newborn Christians. If newborns are going to be healthy and grow to maturity, they must be carefully and loving fed with the truth of the word.

Truth Brings Maturity

The Christian life is a "growing up into Him in all things...until we come to the measure of the stature of the fullness of Christ" (see Eph. 4:13-15). It is important that we place ourselves under pastoral care if we are to "grow up." Even Jesus, who astonished the doctors and lawyers of His time, was entrusted to His parents' care. The Bible says, "Obey thse who rule over you, and be submissive: for they watch out for your souls" (Heb. 13:17). To reject the care of pastoral oversight is to reject God's plan to bring us to Himself and to leave ourselves open to error and the exit from the highway of our journey into the truth.

The ministry that God has given to the Church is five-phased with a threefold purpose. Ephesians 4:11 tells us that God has placed in the church apostles, prophets, evangelists, pastors and teachers. Their purpose is to mature, feed and motivate believers in their own calling and ministry. Only when this equipping is established in the life of the believer will they progress from spiritual newborn to spiritual childhood and on to spiritual adulthood.

In the life of every Christian there must come a point where we "put away childish things" (1 Cor. 13:11). As we become "rooted and grounded" in the basic principles of faith we are "no more children, tossed to and fro, and carried about with every wind of doctrine" (Eph. 4:14). As we grow and mature in the faith we are able to rise above our own problems and trials and reach out with power and confidence to minister the truth to the needs of those around us.

How the Accelerated Christian Training Series Works

The Accelerated Christian Training Series has been designed to meet the crucial need for intensive training in the basic doctrines of the Christian faith. These doctrines are revealed in the context of relationship between God and man. It is designed as a self-instruction course in which believers can journey at their own pace. You will find review questions at the end of each section of material you have studied that will help you to retain what you've learned.

There is an exercise called "Dig a Little Deeper; Grow a Little Closer" at the end of each major section. These reflective questions are designed to help you synthesize the truths you have been taught and then apply them in a personal way. You will be invited to journal throughout the study of this book to provide you with a record of your new understanding and growth in God. Journaling will help you to grow in your ability to hear God's voice and adjust your life and understanding to His purpose.

Following this **A.C.T.S.** course will stimulate and accelerate your spiritual understanding and bring you to a more intimate knowledge of the Truth, who is Jesus Christ. We pray that you will grow in the awareness of the Lord's presence as He guides you to Himself through the study of His Word.

Two Companions for the Road

During this time of new growth in your spiritual life there will be questions that come to mind. You will meet two companions throughout this series on the road to truth. They are Newly Newborn and Truly Taughtright. Newly will ask some of the same questions that you ask, and Truly, his mentor, will give the answers.

The New Covenant

Throughout the previous sections we learned that God extended many invitations to man to bring him back into the intimate trust and fellowship that he once enjoyed with his Creator. Adam, who chose to doubt and to disobey God, was separated from God and hopelessly alone. But God, who is faithful, loving and compassionate, would not leave man in this state of separation. God revealed His deep desire for restoration through covenants made with men like Noah, Abraham, and David. With each new covenant came the promise of restoration but also bitter disappointment, as man was never able to live in perfect faith and obedience toward God.

In the various covenants of the Old Testament we see that not only did God continue His calling of man, but expanded it to greater and greater numbers of people. First God dealt with a single man, Adam. Then God dealt with the single family of Noah, and then God established a covenant with a family that became the nation of Israel. Each covenant contained greater revelation of the Person and promises of God. What could follow but that the whole world should be called into covenant relationship with God?

But how would a whole world of strangers ever be able to live in faith and obedience toward a holy God when no man had ever done so? God would have to bring about a whole different kind of covenant to restore the innocence that Adam once enjoyed with God. God sent His only Son, Jesus, God in the flesh, to live in perfect faith and perfect obedience to His Father. Those in the Old Testament tried to live in faith and obedience to God but possessed a doubting and disobedient nature. If intimate oneness between God and man was to be restored then it would require a new nature. So God, through the perfect and sinless life of Jesus Christ, offers man a new nature; one that would be led by the Spirit of God rather than the independent and rebellious urges of the natural man.

This was what Jeremiah meant when he wrote, *"But this is the covenant that I will make with the house of Israel after those days, says the Lord: I will put My law in their minds, and write it on their hearts; and I will be their God, and they shall be My people"* (Jer. 31:33). Under this New Covenant, man, who was spiritually dead, became spiritually alive to God.

As we walk through this section on the New Covenant and its "go between," Jesus Christ, we will see that we receive a new nature by which we can live in intimate fellowship with God. Once again we can live in faith and obedience, through the Son of God. Keep the following verses in mind as you learn more about this New Covenant.

> *And He died for all, that those who live should live no longer for themselves, but for Him who died for them and rose again…Therefore, if anyone is in Christ, he is a new creation; old things have passed away; behold, all things have become new* (2 Corinthians 5:15,17).

> *I have been crucified with Christ; it is no longer I who live, but Christ lives in me; and the life which I now live in the flesh I live by faith in the Son of God, who loved me and gave Himself for me* (Galatians 2:20).

I. The New Covenant

A. What Is the New Covenant?

1. The New Covenant is the agreement that God offers to all men to restore right relationship through the Person of Jesus Christ, His Son.

For this is My blood of the new covenant, which is shed for many for the remission of sins (Matthew 26:28).

And Christ himself is the means by which our sins are forgiven, and not our sins only, but also the sins of everyone (1 John 2:2 TEV).

2. The New Covenant was written about by the prophets who lived under the Old Covenant.

Behold, the days are coming, says the Lord, when I will make a new covenant with the house of Israel and with the house of Judah—not according to the covenant that I made with their fathers in the day that I took them by the hand to lead them out of the land of Egypt, My covenant which they broke, though I was a husband to them, says the Lord. But this is the covenant that I will make with the house of Israel after those days, says the Lord: I will put My law in their minds, and write it on their hearts; and I will be their God, and they shall be My people (Jeremiah 31:31-33).

3.   The New Covenant abolished the Old Covenant because Israel was not able to keep it.

For if that first covenant had been faultless, then no place would have been sought for a second. Because finding fault with them, He says: "Behold, the days are coming, says the Lord, when I will make a new covenant with the house of Israel and with the house of Judah" (Hebrews 8:7-8).

4.   The New Covenant fulfills the purpose of God, which is to take away sin and restore righteous relationship.

How much more shall the blood of Christ, who through the eternal Spirit offered Himself without spot to God, cleanse your conscience from dead works to serve the living God? And for this reason He is the Mediator of the new covenant, by means of death, for the redemption of the transgressions under the first covenant, that those who are called may receive the promise of the eternal inheritance. He then would have had to suffer often since the foundation of the world; but now, once at the end of the ages, He has appeared to put away sin by the sacrifice of Himself (Hebrews 9:14-15,26).

B.   **Who Is the Mediator of This New Covenant?**

1.   Jesus Christ is the Mediator, the One who brings man back into fellowship with God.

For I received from the Lord that which I also delivered to you: that the Lord Jesus on the same night in which He was betrayed took bread; and when He had given thanks, He broke it and said, "Take, eat; this is My body which is broken for you; do this in remembrance of Me." In the same manner He also took the cup after supper, saying, "This cup is the new covenant in My blood. This do, as often as you drink it, in remembrance of Me" (1 Corinthians 11:23-25).

For there is one God and one Mediator between God and men, the Man Christ Jesus (1 Timothy 2:5).

But now He has obtained a more excellent ministry, inasmuch as He is also Mediator of a better covenant, which was established on better promises (Hebrews 8:6).

2.   It is the blood of Jesus that guarantees the New Covenant.

By so much more Jesus has become a surety of a better covenant (Hebrews 7:22).

Not with the blood of goats and calves, but with His own blood He entered the Most Holy Place once for all, having obtained eternal redemption. For if the blood of bulls and goats and the ashes of a heifer, sprinkling the unclean, sanctifies for the purifying of the flesh, how much more shall the blood of Christ, who through the eternal Spirit offered Himself without spot to God, cleanse your conscience from dead works to serve the living God? And for this reason He is the Mediator of the new covenant, by means of death, for the redemption of the transgressions under the first covenant, that those who are called may receive the promise of the eternal inheritance (Hebrews 9:12-15).

Therefore, brethren, having boldness to enter the Holiest by the blood of Jesus, by a new and living way which He consecrated for us, through the veil, that is, His flesh (Hebrews 10:19-20).

C. Where Do We Read About the New Covenant?

We read about the New Covenant in the second part of the Bible called the New Testament.

— In the Gospels of Matthew, Mark, Luke, and John we read about the life and ministry of Jesus Christ.

— In the Book of Acts we read about the beginnings of the Church.

— In the Epistles we read about various issues and doctrines the apostles encountered in the new churches.

— In the Book of Revelation we read prophesies and warnings to the Church.

14

D. How Do We Enter Into the New Covenant?

1. We enter into the New Covenant through repentance—turning away from our old self-centered and sinful ways—and turning in faith to Jesus Christ.

"Therefore let all the house of Israel know for certain that God has made Him both Lord and Christ—this Jesus whom you crucified." Now when they heard this they were pierced to the heart, and said to Peter and the rest of the apostles, "Brethren, what shall we do?" Peter said to them, "Repent, and each of you be baptized in the name of Jesus Christ for the forgiveness of your sins; and you will receive the gift of the Holy Spirit" (Acts 2:36-38 NAS).

But what does it say? "The word is near you, in your mouth and in your heart"—that is, the word of faith which we are preaching, that if you confess with your mouth Jesus as Lord, and believe in your heart that God raised Him from the dead, you will be saved; for with the heart a person believes, resulting in righteousness, and with the mouth he confesses, resulting in salvation. For the Scripture says, "Whoever believes in Him will not be disappointed" (Romans 10:8-11 NAS).

2. We enter the covenant by receiving the sign of the New Covenant, which is baptism.

For I will take you from the nations, gather you from all the lands and bring you into your own land. Then I will sprinkle clean water on you, and you will be clean; I will cleanse you from all your filthiness and from all your idols. Moreover, I will give you a new heart and put a new spirit within you; and I will remove the heart of stone from your flesh and give you a heart of flesh. I will put My Spirit within you and cause you to walk in My statutes, and you will be careful to observe My ordinances (Ezekiel 36:24-27 NAS).

Or do you not know that all of us who have been baptized into Christ Jesus have been baptized into His death? Therefore we have been buried with Him through baptism into death, so that as Christ was raised from the dead through the glory of the Father, so we too might walk in newness of life. For if we have become united with Him in the likeness of His death, certainly we shall also be in the likeness of His resurrection (Romans 6:3-5 NAS).

And in Him you were also circumcised with a circumcision made without hands, in the removal of the body of the flesh by the circumcision of Christ; having been buried with Him in baptism, in which you were also raised up with Him through faith in the working of God, who raised Him from the dead (Colossians 2:11-12 NAS).

Let's Review What We Have Learned About the New Covenant.

1.   The New Covenant is the _____ that God offers to all men to restore right _____ through the Person of Jesus Christ, His Son.

2. *I will put My law in their* _____, *and write it on their* _____; *and I will be their God, and they shall be My people* (Jeremiah 31:33b).

3. It is the _____ of Jesus that guarantees the New Covenant.

4. Along with the New Covenant we receive a new _____ that wants to obey the Spirit of God.

5. How do we enter into the New Covenant?

_____

_____

_____

6. What does the word *repentance* mean?

_____

_____

_____

_____

Dig a Little Deeper; Grow a Little Closer

1. Read the verses below and respond to the discussion questions.

For as many as are led by the Spirit of God, these are sons of God. For you did not receive the spirit of bondage again to fear, but you received the Spirit of adoption by whom we cry out, "Abba, Father." The

Spirit Himself bears witness with our spirit that we are children of God (Romans 8:14-16).

2.   These verses are a description of the new nature that we receive when we are born again and enter into the kingdom of God. What effect does this "spirit of adoption" have on the way we are able to walk in obedience to our heavenly Father?

_____

_____

_____

3.   Are there areas of your life that are governed by fear of judgment rather than your relationship to God as His child? Lift those areas of fear to your loving "Abba" in prayer.

_____

_____

_____

Review Notes

The New Covenant

The New Covenant

The New Covenant

II. The Person of Jesus Christ

A. Who Is Jesus Christ?

1. Jesus Christ is both the Son of God and the Son of man.

Concerning His Son Jesus Christ our Lord, who was born of the seed of David according to the flesh, and declared to be the Son of God with power according to the Spirit of holiness, by the resurrection from the dead (Romans 1:3-4).

2. Jesus Christ is the only way of salvation for man.

For God so loved the world that He gave His only begotten Son, that whoever believes in Him should not perish but have everlasting life. For God did not send His Son into the world to condemn the world, but that the world through Him might be saved (John 3:16-17).

Let it be known to you all, and to all the people of Israel, that by the name of Jesus Christ of Nazareth, whom you crucified, whom God raised from the dead, by Him this man stands here before you whole...Nor is there salvation in any other, for there is no other name under heaven given among men by which we must be saved (Acts 4:10,12).

3. Jesus Christ is the Messiah of Israel. The name *Jesus* means "Yahweh is salvation." His name *Christ* means the "anointed one."

And she will bring forth a Son, and you shall call His name Jesus, for He will save His people from their sins (Matthew 1:21).

The Spirit of the Lord is upon Me, because He has anointed Me to preach the gospel to the poor; He has sent Me to heal the brokenhearted, to proclaim liberty to the captives and recovery of sight to the blind, to set at liberty those who are oppressed; to proclaim the acceptable year of the Lord (Luke 4:18-19).

...God anointed Jesus of Nazareth with the Holy Spirit and with power, who went about doing good and healing all who were oppressed by the devil, for God was with Him (Acts 10:38).

B.   Why Must We Understand the Person of Jesus?

1.   We must understand the Person of Jesus because He is the very source of Christianity.

I am the vine, you are the branches. He who abides in Me, and I in him, bears much fruit; for without Me you can do nothing (John 15:5).

Now you are the body of Christ, and members individually (1 Corinthians 12:27).

2.   We must understand the Person of Jesus because without Him there is no Christianity. We cannot separate Jesus from His teaching.

And if Christ is not risen, then our preaching is empty and your faith is also empty (1 Corinthians 15:14).

Nor is there salvation in any other, for there is no other name under heaven given among men by which we must be saved (Acts 4:12).

Let's Review What We Have Learned About the Person of Jesus.

1. Jesus Christ is both the Son of _____ and the Son of _____.

2. *For God so loved the world that He gave His only begotten _____, that whoever _____ in Him should not perish but have everlasting life* (John 3:16).

3. Jesus Christ is the _____ of Israel.

4. We must understand the Person of Jesus because He is the very _____ of Christianity.

Dig a Little Deeper; Grow a Little Closer

1. Read the following verses and respond to the discussion questions.

The Spirit of the Lord is upon Me, because He has anointed Me to preach the gospel to the poor; He has sent Me to heal the brokenhearted, to proclaim liberty to the captives and recovery of sight to the blind, to set at liberty those who are oppressed; to proclaim the acceptable year of the Lord (Luke 4:18-19).

2. List the activities that Jesus has been anointed to perform in your life according to this text.

_____

_____

_____

_____

3. Think of places in your life that you carry wounds from the past, where you feel bound, or oppressed, or in need of physical healing. Jesus has been anointed to minister to those areas. List any of these where you desire the anointing of Christ to flow over you.

_____

_____

_____

_____

4. Now, realizing that you are the vessel of God to carry that same anointing to others, ask the Lord to bring to mind anyone

you know who needs that same anointing and bring it to them. List their name and needs below. Make it a point to minister to them.

_____

_____

_____

_____

Review Notes

_____

_____

_____

_____

_____

_____

_____

_____

_____

_____

_____

_____

_____

_____

_____

_____

_____

_____

_____

_____

_____

_____

_____

The Person of Jesus Christ

The Person of Jesus Christ

The New Covenant

_____

_____

_____

_____

_____

_____

_____

_____

_____

_____

_____

_____

_____

_____

_____

_____

_____

_____

_____

_____

_____

_____

_____

The Person of Jesus Christ

III. The Nature of Jesus Christ

A. **What Two Natures Are United Only in Jesus Christ?**

1. Jesus Christ was fully human. He was God incarnate (in the flesh).

Behold, the virgin shall be with child, and bear a Son, and they shall call His name Immanuel, which is translated, "God with us" (Matthew 1:23).

And behold, you will conceive in your womb and bring forth a Son, and shall call His name Jesus (Luke 1:31).

And the Word became flesh and dwelt among us, and we beheld His glory, the glory as of the only begotten of the Father, full of grace and truth (John 1:14).

For what the law could not do in that it was weak through the flesh, God did by sending His own Son in the likeness of sinful flesh, on account of sin: He condemned sin in the flesh (Romans 8:3).

2. Jesus Christ was fully God. He was called the Son of God.

God has fulfilled this for us their children, in that He has raised up Jesus. As it is also written in the second Psalm: "You are My Son, today I have begotten You" (Acts 13:33).

But Jesus kept silent. And the high priest answered and said to Him, "I put You under oath by the living God: Tell us if You are the Christ, the Son of God!" Jesus said to him, "It is as you said. Nevertheless, I say to you, hereafter you will see the Son of Man sitting at the right hand of the Power, and coming on the clouds of heaven" (Matthew 26:63-64).

The beginning of the gospel of Jesus Christ, the Son of God (Mark 1:1).

And the unclean spirits, whenever they saw Him, fell down before Him and cried out, saying, "You are the Son of God" (Mark 3:11).

3. Only in Jesus do these two natures, divinity and humanity, unite.

For God so loved the world that He gave His only begotten Son, that whoever believes in Him should not perish but have everlasting life (John 3:16).

No one has seen God at any time. The only begotten Son, who is in the bosom of the Father, He has declared Him (John 1:18).

In this the love of God was manifested toward us, that God has sent His only begotten Son into the world, that we might live through Him (1 John 4:9).

B. How Do We Know That Jesus Christ Was Man?

1. We know that Jesus was man because He was born of a woman.

Now the birth of Jesus Christ was as follows: After His mother Mary was betrothed to Joseph, before they came together, she was found with child of the Holy Spirit (Matthew 1:18).

But when the fullness of the time had come, God sent forth His Son, born of a woman, born under the law (Galatians 4:4).

2.   We know that Jesus was man because He grew and developed like any other human.

And the Child grew and became strong in spirit, filled with wisdom; and the grace of God was upon Him. And Jesus increased in wisdom and stature, and in favor with God and men (Luke 2:40,52).

3.   We know that Jesus was man because He had human flesh and appearance.

And the Word became flesh and dwelt among us, and we beheld His glory, the glory as of the only begotten of the Father, full of grace and truth (John 1:14).

Then the woman of Samaria said to Him, "How is it that You, being a Jew, ask a drink from me, a Samaritan woman?" For Jews have no dealings with Samaritans (John 4:9).

For He shall grow up before Him as a tender plant, and as a root out of dry ground. He has no form or comeliness; and when we see Him, there is no beauty that we should desire Him (Isaiah 53:2).

4.   We know that Jesus was man because He had human needs and emotions.

And when He had fasted forty days and forty nights, afterward He was hungry (Matthew 4:2).

And suddenly a great tempest arose on the sea, so that the boat was covered with the waves. But He was asleep (Matthew 8:24).

After this, Jesus, knowing that all things were now accomplished, that the Scripture might be fulfilled, said, "I thirst!" (John 19:28)

Now Jacob's well was there. Jesus therefore, being wearied from His journey, sat thus by the well. It was about the sixth hour (John 4:6).

5.   We know that Jesus was man because He had a human name.

C.   How Do We Know That Jesus Christ Is God?

1.   We know that Jesus is God because He was given divine titles:

—   **God**

In the beginning was the Word, and the Word was with God, and the Word was God (John 1:1).

And Thomas answered and said to Him, "My Lord and my God!" (John 20:28)

—   **Son of God**

Then those who were in the boat came and worshiped Him, saying, "Truly You are the Son of God" (Matthew 14:33).

Then a voice came from heaven, "You are My beloved Son, in whom I am well pleased" (Mark 1:11).

So when the centurion, who stood opposite Him, saw that He cried out like this and breathed His last, he said, "Truly this Man was the Son of God!" (Mark 15:39)

— **Lord**

For there is born to you this day in the city of David a Savior, who is Christ the Lord (Luke 2:11).

The word which God sent to the children of Israel, preaching peace through Jesus Christ—He is Lord of all (Acts 10:36).

— **Immanuel**

Behold, the virgin shall be with child, and bear a Son, and they shall call His name Immanuel, which is translated, "God with us" (Matthew 1:23).

— **Holy One**

For You will not leave my soul in Sheol, nor will You allow Your Holy One to see corruption (Psalm 16:10).

Now there was a man in their synagogue with an unclean spirit. And he cried out, saying, "Let us alone! What have we to do with You, Jesus of Nazareth? Did You come to destroy us? I know who You are—the Holy One of God!" (Mark 1:23-24)

2.   We know that Jesus is God because of the unique qualities that belonged to Him:

— **He is omniscient.**

Now we are sure that You know all things, and have no need that anyone should question You. By this we believe that You came forth from God (John 16:30).

— **He is omnipotent.**

And Jesus came and spoke to them, saying, "All authority has been given to Me in heaven and on earth" (Matthew 28:18).

— **He is eternal.**

In the beginning was the Word, and the Word was with God, and the Word was God. He was in the beginning with God (John 1:1-2).

Jesus said to them, "Most assuredly, I say to you, before Abraham was, I AM" (John 8:58).

— **He is unchangeable.**

Jesus Christ is the same yesterday, today, and forever (Hebrews 13:8).

3. We know that Jesus is God because He does the works of God.

— **He is the Creator.**

All things were made through Him, and without Him nothing was made that was made (John 1:3).

For by Him all things were created that are in heaven and that are on earth, visible and invisible, whether thrones or dominions or principalities or powers. All things were created through Him and for Him. And He is before all things, and in Him all things consist (Colossians 1:16-17).

— **He forgives sins.**

"For which is easier, to say, 'Your sins are forgiven you,' or to say, 'Arise and walk'? But that you may know that the Son of Man has power on earth to forgive sins"—then He said to the paralytic, "Arise, take up your bed, and go to your house" (Matthew 9:5-6).

Then He said to her, "Your sins are forgiven" (Luke 7:48).

— **He judges man.**

For the Father judges no one, but has committed all judgment to the Son (John 5:22).

I charge you therefore before God and the Lord Jesus Christ, who will judge the living and the dead at His appearing and His kingdom (2 Timothy 4:1).

Because He has appointed a day on which He will judge the world in righteousness by the Man whom He has ordained. He has given assurance of this to all by raising Him from the dead (Acts 17:31).

4.   We know that Jesus is God because He was worshiped as God.

— **By Thomas the disciple**

And Thomas answered and said to Him, "My Lord and my God!" (John 20:28)

— By the other disciples

Then those who were in the boat came and worshiped Him, saying, "Truly You are the Son of God" (Matthew 14:33).

And they worshiped Him, and returned to Jerusalem with great joy (Luke 24:52).

— By the psalmist

So the King will greatly desire your beauty; because He is your Lord, worship Him (Psalm 45:11).

5. We know that Jesus is God because He displayed sovereignty and authority.

I will declare the decree: the Lord has said to Me, "You are My Son, today I have begotten You. Ask of Me, and I will give You the nations for Your inheritance, and the ends of the earth for Your possession" (Psalm 2:7-8).

You have heard that it was said...But I say to you... (Matthew 5:21-22).

And Jesus came and spoke to them, saying, "All authority has been given to Me in heaven and on earth" (Matthew 28:18).

D. Why Is It Important That Jesus Is Fully God?

1. Jesus had to be fully God because only God could carry the burden of God's wrath.

None of them can by any means redeem his brother, nor give to God a ransom for him—for the redemption of their souls is costly, and it shall cease forever (Psalm 49:7-8).

Knowing that you were not redeemed with corruptible things, like silver or gold, from your aimless conduct received by tradition from your fathers, but with the precious blood of Christ, as of a lamb without blemish and without spot (1 Peter 1:18-19).

For Christ also suffered once for sins, the just for the unjust, that He might bring us to God, being put to death in the flesh but made alive by the Spirit (1 Peter 3:18).

And they sang a new song, saying: "You are worthy to take the scroll, and to open its seals; for You were slain, and have redeemed us to God by Your blood out of every tribe and tongue and people and nation" (Revelation 5:9).

2. Jesus had to be fully God because only God could save man.

But I will sacrifice to You with the voice of thanksgiving; I will pay what I have vowed. Salvation is of the Lord (Jonah 2:9).

Salvation belongs to the Lord. Your blessing is upon Your people (Psalm 3:8).

And crying out with a loud voice, saying, "Salvation belongs to our God who sits on the throne, and to the Lamb!" (Revelation 7:10)

3. Jesus had to be fully God to be Mediator between God and man to bring us back to God.

For there is one God and one Mediator between God and men, the Man Christ Jesus (1 Timothy 2:5).

Therefore He is also able to save to the uttermost those who come to God through Him, since He always lives to make intercession for them (Hebrews 7:25).

E. **Why Is It Important That Jesus Was Fully Human?**

1. Jesus had to be fully human in order to demonstrate the perfect faith and obedience that had been lost at the fall of Adam. Jesus was referred to as the second Adam.

Therefore, just as through one man sin entered the world, and death through sin, and thus death spread to all men, because all sinned...Therefore, as through one man's offense judgment came to all men, resulting in condemnation, even so through one Man's righteous act the free gift came to all men, resulting in justification of life. For as by one man's disobedience many were made sinners, so also by one Man's obedience many will be made righteous (Romans 5:12,18-19).

2. Jesus had to be fully human to be a sympathetic High Priest for us.

45

For we do not have a High Priest who cannot sympathize with our weaknesses, but was in all points tempted as we are, yet without sin. Let us therefore come boldly to the throne of grace, that we may obtain mercy and find grace to help in time of need (Hebrews 4:15-16).

3.   Jesus had to be fully human in order to die as a substitute sacrifice for man.

Just as the Son of Man did not come to be served, but to serve, and to give His life a ransom for many (Matthew 20:28).

Whom God set forth as a propitiation by His blood, through faith, to demonstrate His righteousness, because in His forbearance God had passed over the sins that were previously committed (Romans 3:25).

And He Himself is the propitiation for our sins, and not for ours only but also for the whole world (1 John 2:2).

But we see Jesus, who was made a little lower than the angels, for the suffering of death crowned with glory and honor, that He, by the grace of God, might taste death for everyone…For indeed He does not give aid to angels, but He does give aid to the seed of Abraham. Therefore, in all things He had to be made like His brethren, that He might be a merciful and faithful High Priest in things pertaining to God, to make propitiation for the sins of the people (Hebrews 2:9,16-17).

F. For What Three Offices Was Jesus Christ Anointed?

1. Jesus was anointed as Prophet to reveal to us the nature of God through the Word of God.

The Spirit of the Lord is upon Me, because He has anointed Me to preach the gospel to the poor; He has sent Me to heal the brokenhearted, to proclaim liberty to the captives and recovery of sight to the blind, to set at liberty those who are oppressed; to proclaim the acceptable year of the Lord (Luke 4:18-19).

And He said to them, "What things?" So they said to Him, "The things concerning Jesus of Nazareth, who was a Prophet mighty in deed and word before God and all the people" (Luke 24:19).

For He whom God has sent speaks the words of God, for God does not give the Spirit by measure (John 3:34).

For Moses truly said to the fathers, "The Lord your God will raise up for you a Prophet like me from your brethren. Him you shall hear in all things, whatever He says to you" (Acts 3:22).

2. Jesus was anointed as Priest as He went to the cross to present Himself as a sacrifice to satisfy the justice of God. He restores our relationship with God and then becomes our intercessor at the throne.

Seeing then that we have a great High Priest who has passed through the heavens, Jesus the Son of God, let us hold fast our confession. For we do not have a High Priest who cannot sympathize with our weaknesses, but was in all points tempted as we are, yet without sin (Hebrews 4:14-15).

But He, because He continues forever, has an unchangeable priesthood (Hebrews 7:24).

Now this is the main point of the things we are saying: We have such a High Priest, who is seated at the right hand of the throne of the Majesty in the heavens, a Minister of the sanctuary and of the true tabernacle which the Lord erected, and not man (Hebrews 8:1-2).

How much more shall the blood of Christ, who through the eternal Spirit offered Himself without spot to God, cleanse your conscience from dead works to serve the living God? (Hebrews 9:14)

3.   Jesus was anointed as King to rule over His people and to destroy the power of the enemy.

The Lord said to my Lord, "Sit at My right hand, till I make Your enemies Your footstool." The Lord shall send the rod of Your strength out of Zion. Rule in the midst of Your enemies! (Psalm 110:1-2)

Behold, the Lord God shall come with a strong hand, and His arm shall rule for Him; behold, His reward is with Him, and His work before Him (Isaiah 40:10).

Behold, My Servant shall deal prudently; he shall be exalted and extolled and be very high (Isaiah 52:13).

And Jesus came and spoke to them, saying, "All authority has been given to Me in heaven and on earth" (Matthew 28:18).

Who has gone into heaven and is at the right hand of God, angels and authorities and powers having been made subject to Him (1 Peter 3:22).

Let's Review What We Have Learned About the Nature of Jesus Christ.

1. He was God incarnate, which means _____.

2. Only in Jesus do these two natures, _____ and _____, unite.

3.   List three titles that were ascribed to Jesus that tell us He was God.

_____

_____

_____

4.   List three unique qualities that belonged to Jesus and two works that tell us He was God.

_____

_____

_____

_____

_____

_____

5.   Jesus had to be fully human so that He could be a sympathetic _____.

6.   Jesus had to be fully human in order to demonstrate the perfect _____ and _____ that had been lost at the fall of Adam. Jesus was referred to as the second _____.

7.   For what three offices was Jesus anointed?

_____

_____

_____

_____

Dig a Little Deeper; Grow a Little Closer

1. Read the following verses and respond to the following questions.

> *For we do not have a High Priest who cannot sympathize with our weaknesses, but was in all points tempted as we are, yet without sin. Let us therefore come boldly to the throne of grace, that we may obtain mercy and find grace to help in time of need* (Hebrews 4:15-16).

2. Are there times when you struggle with sin or suffering that you feel alone and without God? What do these verses tell us about the kind of High Priest Jesus is?

_____

3. Realize that even while you are reading these words that Jesus is standing at the throne of God on your behalf. How will this reality affect your prayer life and your attitude toward difficulties?

_____

_____

_____

Review Notes

The Nature of Jesus Christ

The New Covenant

The Nature of Jesus Christ

The New Covenant

The Nature of Jesus Christ

IV.   The Humiliation of Jesus Christ

A.   **How Did Jesus Christ Humble Himself?**

1.   Jesus humbled Himself by emptying Himself of His power and position in Heaven.

For you know the grace of our Lord Jesus Christ, that though He was rich, yet for your sakes He became poor, that you through His poverty might become rich (2 Corinthians 8:9).

But made Himself of no reputation, taking the form of a bondservant, and coming in the likeness of men (Philippians 2:7).

2.   Jesus humbled Himself by being born of a woman in a stable.

Therefore the Lord Himself will give you a sign: Behold, the virgin shall conceive and bear a Son, and shall call His name Immanuel (Isaiah 7:14).

And she brought forth her firstborn Son, and wrapped him in swaddling cloths, and laid Him in a manger, because there was no room for them in the inn (Luke 2:7).

3.   Jesus humbled Himself by being under the law as all other men.

He is despised and rejected by men, a Man of sorrows and acquainted with grief. And we hid, as it were, our faces from Him; He was despised, and we did not esteem Him (Isaiah 53:3).

Christ has redeemed us from the curse of the law, having become a curse for us (for it is written,

"Cursed is everyone who hangs on a tree") (Galatians 3:13).

4.　Jesus humbled Himself by living with poverty and suffering.

And Jesus said to him, "Foxes have holes and birds of the air have nests, but the Son of Man has nowhere to lay His head" (Matthew 8:20).

And He took with Him Peter and the two sons of Zebedee, and He began to be sorrowful and deeply distressed (Matthew 26:37).

5.　Jesus humbled Himself by being persecuted by men and forsaken by God.

He was oppressed and He was afflicted, yet He opened not His mouth; He was led as a lamb to the slaughter, and as a sheep before its shearers is silent, so He opened not His mouth (Isaiah 53:7).

Then they spat in His face and beat Him; and others struck Him with the palms of their hands (Matthew 26:67).

And about the ninth hour Jesus cried out with a loud voice, saying, "Eli, Eli, lama sabachthani?" that is, "My God, My God, why have You forsaken Me?" (Matthew 27:46)

Then they spat on Him, and took the reed and struck Him on the head. And when they had mocked Him, they took the robe off Him, put His own clothes on Him, and led Him away to be crucified (Matthew 27:30-31).

6.　Jesus humbled Himself by suffering crucifixion, taking upon Himself the sins of man and the wrath of God.

*Then they crucified Him, and divided His gar-
ments, casting lots, that it might be fulfilled which
was spoken by the prophet: "They divided My garments among them, and for My clothing they cast
lots"* (Matthew 27:35).

*And He, bearing His cross, went out to a place
called the Place of a Skull, which is called in
Hebrew, Golgotha, where they crucified Him, and
two others with Him, one on either side, and Jesus
in the center* (John 19:17-18).

*Christ has redeemed us from the curse of the law,
having become a curse for us (for it is written,
"Cursed is everyone who hangs on a tree")* (Galatians 3:13).

7.   Jesus humbled Himself by death and burial
        for three days.

*For as Jonah was three days and three nights in
the belly of the great fish, so will the Son of Man be
three days and three nights in the heart of the
earth* (Matthew 12:40).

*Now when evening had come, there came a rich
man from Arimathea, named Joseph, who himself
had also become a disciple of Jesus. This man
went to Pilate and asked for the body of Jesus.
Then Pilate commanded the body to be given to
him. When Joseph had taken the body, he wrapped
it in a clean linen cloth, and laid it in his new
tomb which he had hewn out of the rock; and he
rolled a large stone against the door of the tomb,
and departed* (Matthew 27:57-60).

For I delivered unto you first of all that which I also received, how that Christ died for our sins according to the scriptures; and that He was buried, and that He rose again the third day according to the scriptures (1 Corinthians 15:3-4 KJV).

B. **What Are the Results of Christ's Humiliation?**

1. Through the humiliation of Christ we are redeemed, purchased back from the power of sin and satan. Satan had the power of accusation, sickness, fear, and death.

And I will put enmity between you and the woman, and between your seed and her Seed; He shall bruise your head, and you shall bruise His heel (Genesis 3:15).

And He said to them, "I saw satan fall like lightning from heaven" (Luke 10:18).

Now is the judgment of this world; now the ruler of this world will be cast out (John 12:31).

Having disarmed principalities and powers, He made a public spectacle of them, triumphing over them in it (Colossians 2:15).

He who sins is of the devil, for the devil has sinned from the beginning. For this purpose the Son of God was manifested, that He might destroy the works of the devil (1 John 3:8).

2. Through the humiliation of Christ we are redeemed from all sin.

He shall see the labor of His soul, and be satisfied. By His knowledge My righteous Servant shall justify many, for He shall bear their iniquities (Isaiah 53:11).

For as by one man's disobedience many were made sinners, so also by one Man's obedience many will be made righteous (Romans 5:19).

For He made Him who knew no sin to be sin for us, that we might become the righteousness of God in Him (2 Corinthians 5:21).

3.   Through the humiliation of Christ we are redeemed from death.

"O Death, where is your sting? O Hades, where is your victory?" The sting of death is sin, and the strength of sin is the law. But thanks be to God, who gives us the victory through our Lord Jesus Christ (1 Corinthians 15:55-57).

Inasmuch then as the children have partaken of flesh and blood, He Himself likewise shared in the same, that through death He might destroy him who had the power of death, that is, the devil, and release those who through fear of death were all their lifetime subject to bondage (Hebrews 2:14-15).

4.   Through the humiliation of Christ we are redeemed from the curse of the law (the results of our disobedience to the law).

Now we know that whatever the law says, it says to those who are under the law, that every mouth may be stopped, and all the world may become guilty before God (Romans 3:19).

Christ has redeemed us from the curse of the law, having become a curse for us (for it is written, "Cursed is everyone who hangs on a tree") (Galatians 3:13).

For as many as are of the works of the law are under the curse; for it is written, "Cursed is everyone who does not continue in all things which are written in the book of the law, to do them" (Galatians 3:10).

C. How Has Christ Redeemed Us?

1. Christ has redeemed us through His own innocent blood.

In that day a fountain shall be opened for the house of David and for the inhabitants of Jerusalem, for sin and for uncleanness (Zechariah 13:1).

The next day John saw Jesus coming toward him, and said, "Behold! The Lamb of God who takes away the sin of the world!" (John 1:29)

In Him we have redemption through His blood, the forgiveness of sins, according to the riches of His grace (Ephesians 1:7).

Knowing that you were not redeemed with corruptible things, like silver or gold, from your aimless conduct received by tradition from your fathers, but with the precious blood of Christ, as of a lamb without blemish and without spot (1 Peter 1:18-19).

And you know that He was manifested to take away our sins, and in Him there is no sin (1 John 3:5).

2.　　Christ has redeemed us by making atonement for our sin, (at-one-ment), bringing us back into relationship with God.

For He made Him who knew no sin to be sin for us, that we might become the righteousness of God in Him (2 Corinthians 5:21).

He shall see the labor of His soul, and be satisfied. By His knowledge My righteous Servant shall justify many, for He shall bear their iniquities (Isaiah 53:11).

And be found in Him, not having my own righteousness, which is from the law, but that which is through faith in Christ, the righteousness which is from God by faith (Philippians 3:9).

3.   Christ has redeemed us by taking our place and paying our penalty.

Surely He has borne our griefs and carried our sorrows; yet we esteemed Him stricken, smitten by God, and afflicted. But He was wounded for our transgressions, He was bruised for our iniquities; the chastisement for our peace was upon Him, and by His stripes we are healed (Isaiah 53:4-5).

Christ has redeemed us from the curse of the law, having become a curse for us (for it is written, "Cursed is everyone who hangs on a tree") (Galatians 3:13).

Who Himself bore our sins in His own body on the tree, that we, having died to sins, might live for righteousness—by whose stripes you were healed (1 Peter 2:24).

For Christ also suffered once for sins, the just for the unjust, that He might bring us to God, being put to death in the flesh but made alive by the Spirit (1 Peter 3:18).

4.   Christ has redeemed all who accept Him and has condemned all who refuse Him.

"For the Son of Man has come to save that which was lost (Matthew 18:11).

This is a faithful saying and worthy of all acceptance, that Christ Jesus came into the world to save sinners, of whom I am chief (1 Timothy 1:15).

Truly, these times of ignorance God overlooked, but now commands all men everywhere to repent, because He has appointed a day on which He will judge the world in righteousness by the Man whom He has ordained. He has given assurance of this to all by raising Him from the dead (Acts 17:30-31).

Let's Review What We Have Learned About the Humiliation of Jesus Christ.

1.   Jesus humbled Himself by _____ Himself of His _____ and _____ in Heaven.

2.   *Therefore the Lord Himself will give you a sign: Behold, the virgin shall conceive and bear a Son, and shall call His name* _____. [God with us.] (Isaiah 7:14).

3.   Jesus humbled Himself by being under the _____ as all other men.

4.   Jesus humbled Himself by being _____ by men and _____ by God.

5.   Through the humiliation of Christ we are _____ from all sin.

6.   The word *redeemed* means that we have been _____.

7.   Satan had the power of _____, _____, _____ and death, from which we have been redeemed by the blood of Jesus Christ.

8.   Jesus Christ has redeemed us by making _____ for our sin.

9.   Jesus Christ has redeemed us by taking our _____ and paying our _____.

Dig a Little Deeper; Grow a Little Closer

1.   Below is the entire text of Psalm 22. You may recognize the opening words as those that Jesus spoke while He hung from the cross. They described prophetically the events surrounding the crucifixion many years before it took place. Read it and then answer the following questions.

My God, My God, why have You forsaken Me? Why are You so far from helping Me, and from the words of My groaning? O My God, I cry in the daytime, but You do not hear; and in the night season, and am not silent. But You are holy, enthroned in the praises of Israel. Our fathers trusted in You; they trusted, and You delivered them. They cried to You, and were delivered; they trusted in You, and were not ashamed. But I am a worm, and no man; a reproach of men, and despised of the people. All those who see Me ridicule Me; they shoot out the lip, they shake the head, saying, "He trusted in the Lord, let Him rescue Him; let Him deliver Him, since He delights in Him!" But You are He who took Me out of the womb; You made Me trust while on My mother's breasts. I was cast upon You from birth. From My mother's womb You have been My God. Be not far from Me, for trouble is near; for there is none to help. Many bulls have surrounded Me; strong bulls of Bashan have encircled Me. They gape at Me with their mouths, like a raging and roaring lion. I am poured out like water, and all My bones are out of joint; my heart is like wax; it has melted within Me. My strength is dried up like a potsherd, and My tongue clings to My jaws; You have brought Me to the dust of death. For dogs have surrounded Me; the congregation of the wicked has enclosed Me. They pierced My hands and My feet; I can count all My bones. They look and stare at Me. They divide My garments among them, and for My clothing they cast lots. But You, O Lord, do not be far from Me; O My Strength, hasten to help Me! Deliver Me from the sword, my precious life from the power of the dog. Save Me from the lion's mouth and from the horns of the wild oxen! You have answered Me. I will declare Your name to My brethren; in the midst of the assembly I will praise You. You who fear the Lord, praise Him! All you descendants of Jacob, glorify Him, and fear Him, all you offspring of Israel! For He has not despised nor abhorred the affliction of the afflicted; nor has He hidden His face from Him; but when He cried to Him, He heard. My praise shall be of You in the great assembly; I will pay My vows before those who fear Him. The poor shall eat and be satisfied; those who seek Him will praise the Lord. Let your heart live forever! All the ends of the world shall remember and turn to the Lord, and all the families of the nations shall worship before You. For the kingdom is the Lord's, and He rules over the nations. All the prosperous of the earth shall eat and worship; all those who go down to the dust shall bow before Him, even he who cannot keep himself alive. A posterity shall serve Him. It will be recounted of the Lord to the next generation, they will come and declare His righteousness to a people who will be born, that He has done this.

2. What does this Psalm tell us about the suffering and humiliation of Jesus?

_____

_____

_____

_____

_____

3.   What does this Psalm tell us about the perfect faith and obedience of Jesus Christ?

_____

_____

_____

_____

4.   What does this Psalm tell us about the result of the perfect faith and obedience of Jesus Christ? How do they affect you?

_____

_____

_____

_____

_____

Review Notes

The Humiliation of Jesus Christ

The New Covenant

The Humiliation of Jesus Christ

The Humiliation of Jesus Christ

Be sure to enter into the journal in this book how God responds to what you have prayed.

Books in the *Laying the FOUNDATION* Series:

Book 1—The Nature of God

    I.   The Nature of God

    II.   The Bible

    III.   The Creation

Book 2—The Nature of Man

    I.   The Nature of Man

    II.   The Fall of Man

    III.   The Seed of Rebellion Continues

Book 3—A Call to Faith and Obedience

    I.   Abraham: The Father of Faith and Obedience

    II.   Israel: Called to Be the People of God

Book 4—From Covenant to Kingdom

    I.   Taking Possession of the Promises of God

    II.   Establishing the Kingdom

    III.   The Message of the Prophets

    IV.   Restoring the Remnant of Israel

Book 5—The New Covenant

    I.   The New Covenant

    II.   The Person of Jesus Christ

    III.   The Nature of Jesus Christ

    IV.   The Humiliation of Jesus Christ

More Titles
by Dr. Mark Hanby

➤ **YOU HAVE NOT MANY FATHERS**

"My son, give me your heart." So says the proverb, echoing the heart and passion of our Father in heaven. God has spiritual "dads" all over the world whom He has filled with wisdom, knowledge, compassion, and most of all, love for those young in the faith. You do not have to go through your life untrained and unloved; uncared for and forgotten. There are fathers in Christ who are waiting to pour all they have into your heart, as Elijah did for Elisha. "My son, give me your heart."
ISBN 1-56043-166-0

➤ **YOU HAVE NOT MANY FATHERS STUDY GUIDE**
ISBN 0-7684-2036-9

➤ **THE HOUSE THAT GOD BUILT**

Beyond whatever man can desire is a God-given pattern for the life of the Church. Here Dr. Hanby unfolds practical applications from the design of the Tabernacle that allow us to become the house God is building today.
ISBN 1-56043-091-5

➤ **THE HOUSE THAT GOD BUILT STUDY GUIDE**
ISBN 0-7684-2048-2

➤ **THE RENEWING OF THE HOLY GHOST**

Do you need renewal? Everything in the natural, from birds to blood cells, must either undergo a process of renewal or enter into death. Our spiritual life is no different. With this book, your renewal can begin today!
ISBN 1-56043-031-1

➤ **ANOINTING THE UNSANCTIFIED**

The anointing is more than a talented performance or an emotional response. In this book, Dr. Hanby details the essential ingredients of directional relationship that allow the Spirit of God to flow down upon the Body of Christ—and from us to the needs of a dying world.
ISBN 1-56043-071-0

➤ **PERCEIVING THE WHEEL OF GOD**

On the potter's wheel, a lump of clay yields to a necessary process of careful pressure and constant twisting. Similarly, the form of true faith is shaped by a trusting response to God in a suffering situation. This book offers essential understanding for victory through the struggles of life.
ISBN 1-56043-109-1

Available at your local Christian bookstore.

For more information and sample chapters, visit www.destinyimage.com